AMERICA'S HOMEFRONT
AIR WAR

CIVIL AIR PATROL
AGAINST GERMAN SUBMARINES
IN WORLD WAR II

THE UNTOLD FACTS OF ARMED U.S. CIVILIANS
AND THEIR SUCCESSFUL LIGHTPLANE
RETALIATION TO THE INVASION OF
AMERICA'S EAST COAST

FEATURING OVER 90 ILLUSTRATIONS AND PHOTOS

With discussion questions for students and
advanced military roundtables

BY ROGER THIEL

AMERICA'S HOMEFRONT AIR WAR – CIVIL AIR PATROL
AGAINST GERMAN SUBMARINES IN WORLD WAR II –
THE UNTOLD FACTS OF ARMED U.S. CIVILIANS AND
THEIR SUCCESSFUL LIGHTPLANE RETALIATION TO
THE INVASION OF AMERICA'S EAST COAST

www.Americashomefrontairwar.com

Published by

Thiel Press – 1101 14th Street, N.W. • #64 • Washington, D.C. 20005

ISBN **978-0-9976605-2-4**

WASHINGTON, D.C.
Established 1974

TABLE OF CONTENTS

PROLOGUE AND SUMMARY:

(1) TORPEDOINGS OF ALLIED SHIPS
took place in American waters,
sometimes as close as a mile from shore.

PROLOGUE AND SUMMARY

DID THIS U.S. CIVILIAN 'HOME GUARD' DRIVE AWAY AN INVADING ENEMY MILITARY FORCE?

On January 15, 1942, Mr. and Mrs. Homefront America awoke to headlines which shouted: TANKER TORPEDOED 60 MILES OFF LONG ISLAND. The enemy had struck. Six weeks after Pearl Harbor, World War Two had moved from Europe and the Pacific to the nation's front door. In the previous four days, four ships had been sunk in American waters.

America was under attack. Deep in the night, explosions on the sea resounded across the Atlantic shore. Coastal dwellers sometimes saw terrible orange glows on the night horizon and looked on in a dull, helpless group stare. It was the collective shock of an America besieged.

The sinkings in American waters increased from 12 in January to 25 in February. The German submarines were operating in what seemed

---

NOTES ON TERMS AND STYLE:

The official title of CAP's armed campaign against invading German submarines was: Civil Air Patrol Coastal Patrol. The informal term, "CAP anti-sub" is also used throughout this book.

When referring to Civil Air Patrol by its initials, each of the three letters are usually spoken ("C.A.P.") rather than being pronounced as the word "cap."

All military ranks mentioned herein are of the Civil Air Patrol, except as otherwise noted.

(2) GERMAN SUBMARINE
(Type 7 U-boat)

to be a shooting gallery of their own choosing. An enemy of the United
States had placed invasive, armed, attacking troops within eyesight of
New York City.

The strategic implications were harsh. Shipping losses increased
through the spring, threatening Allied ability to counter Axis powers
in Europe and to sustain England's strategic posture as a foothold to
eventually liberate the continent.

The people on shore reacted blankly to these audacious teeth sunk into their heel and faced east to a dark, cold Atlantic. Oil slicks, debris from sinkings, and even bodies of sailors washed up on shore. War had come from "over there" to the American homeland, invading not just the ocean, but decades of their insular security. This enemy was unseen. It operated by stealth. It struck suddenly and randomly, also inflicting a stark alteration onto the group identity of the people. What it meant to be an American was different.

(3) CAP COASTAL PATROL PILOTS "READY TO GO"
Lt. William Hall, Major Ralph Earle (Base Commander),
Capt. Wallace D. Newcomb, Major George H. Miller.
Note bomb placed upright at left.
(CP Base 17, Suffolk, Long Island, New York)

In the aftermath of Pearl Harbor, the greatest country in the world had sailed most of its U.S. Navy to the Pacific as its industry frantically worked to create what would become the "arsenal of democracy." But on the East Coast, on the nation's front door, there was almost no defense. The Atlantic and Gulf coasts had been left severely underguarded.

Meanwhile, the people waited. They waited for their government to do something, to send a Big New Thing to save them. But it was not a Big New Thing that saved them, it was many little ones that performed the job. Citizens may have wished for strong military retaliation, but the day was saved by methodical, undramatic actions. They may have looked for large, warlike weapons to come, but what arrived were machines designed for efficient, peacetime purpose.

America's circumstance had set the stage for an improbable, unique, adapted force, created in the nick of time and uniquely spanning the civilian and the military.

Even today, what happened seems remarkable, almost impossible: a civilian force was substantially responsible for driving a potent military invader away from American waters. Flying armed missions out over the ocean, they established a presence countering the enemy, and, in a summit of civilian efficiency performing military actions, contributed what probably became the majority energy to repel them.

The Civil Air Patrol could be too easily dismissed as a well-meaning harassment force, and yet in 1947, Henry H. "Hap" Arnold, Commanding General of the U.S. Army Air Forces, would write: "For one period – at the start of the war – CAP was the only agency that was able to take any real action toward controlling the submarine menace."

Although they had few actual interactions with enemy subs, and their overwhelming value was as a deterrent force, the Civil Air Patrol Coastal Patrol affected the global strategies of a world at war. The CAP influenced the tactics of U-boats and therefore the safety of merchant shipping, exerting a serious influence, possibly a pivotal one, to a world at war.

Here are the facts of how they did it.

————

CIVIL AIR PATROL
WWII Coastal Patrol/Anti-Submarine Bases

25th ANTI-SUBMARINE WING

BASE

20	BAR HARBOR, MAINE
19	PORTLAND, MAINE
18	FALMOUTH (Cape Cod), MASSACHUSETTS
17	SUFFOLK (Long Island), NEW YORK
1	ATLANTIC CITY, NEW JERSEY
2	REHOBOTH BEACH, DELAWARE
4	PARKSLEY, VIRGINIA
16	MANTEO, NORTH CAROLINA
21	BEAUFORT, NORTH CAROLINA
8	CHARLESTON (St. James Isle), SOUTH CAROLINA
6	BRUNSWICK (St. Simon's Island), GEORGIA

26th ANTI-SUBMARINE WING

BASE

5	FLAGLER BEACH, FLORIDA
3	LANTANA, FLORIDA
7	MIAMI, FLORIDA
13	SARASOTA, FLORIDA
14	PANAMA CITY, FLORIDA
11	PASCAGOULA, MISSISSIPPI
9	GRAND ISLE, LOUISIANA
10	BEAUMONT, TEXAS
15	CORPUS CHRISTI, TEXAS
12	BROWNSVILLE, TEXAS

(Bases numbered by activation sequence, 1942)

WASHINGTON

ATLANTIC OCEAN

Gulf of Mexico

THE BAHAMAS

NASSAU

(4) MAP OF 21 COASTAL PATROL BASES
(see p. 92 for exact activation dates)

CAP COASTAL PATROL

Since the late 1930s, Gill Robb Wilson, New Jersey State Aviation Director, and other leading aviators of the day, had sensed possible encroachment by an enemy in the event of war. They created a plan by which U.S. civilian pilots and their airplanes might relieve the regular military of patrolling the east coast. They pressed the case which resulted in the formation of the Civil Air Patrol on December 1, 1941.

December 1, 1941: the CAP had been willed into existence only six days before Pearl Harbor. If not for those earlier years of foresight, the CAP might never have existed at all.

The first three Civil Air Patrol bases were an experiment presented to a speculative U.S. military. They began flying overwater almost as soon as they arrived at their Atlantic coastal locations. In early March, unarmed CAP fliers from Base Two in Delaware encountered an enemy submarine. They spotted what they first thought was a sinking tanker wallowing in the water. But it was a U-boat, already crash diving after seeing their airplane approach. In the first three CAP patrol areas, sinkings reduced. More anti-sub bases were authorized and quickly activated.

As the Spring of 1942 progressed, overall sinkings in U.S. waters increased from 25 in February to an horrific 52 in May. In April, Florida CAP pilots encountered a U-boat which attempted to flee from them and became stranded. The unarmed crew circled it until the submarine got away. However, because of this incident, in the late spring and early summer of 1942, most CAP bases were given bombs and depth charges. By June, with eight CAP bases in operation, the sinkings reduced to 35.

By September 1942, as its 21st and final base was activated, CAP covered America's Atlantic and Gulf coasts, extending from Maine to Texas. During this entire period, the regular military reportedly did not increase its patrols. However, by September, sinkings had reduced to almost none.

(5) BASE 17 AIRCRAFT RAMP
Aircraft types pictured here include: Sikorsky S-39 rescue amphibian,
Waco cabin biplane, Stinson Voyager, Fairchild 24.
Many other civilian cabin aircraft types, not pictured herein, were used by the 21 Bases
of CAP Coastal Patrol, including: Cessna Airmaster, Beech Staggerwing, Bellanca,
Rearwin Cloudster, Monocoupe, and others.
(CP Base 17, Suffolk, New York)

Although there was a blackout on civilian flying within 100 miles
of the coast, CAP bases were an exception to this, and were a cross section
of U.S. civil aviation. They creatively adapted their civilian airplanes to
carry military weapons. One pilot, operating off a grass runway with a
200 pound bomb, recalled, "I flew the most careful takeoffs and landings
of my life." Based on availability of munitions, it was possible for an
overwater patrol plane to remain unarmed.

CAP anti-sub personnel signed contracts for three months, six months, or "for the duration." They wore a patch with the letters "US." In case they ditched and were picked up by the enemy, this patch meant they would be treated as soldiers and not as spies. Underscoring their signature uniqueness, CAP personnel were the only civilians permitted to wear this insignia. Many pilots didn't meet military age or physical requirements. The CAP's ranks included veterans who had flown against Germans in World War One.

Rank was given sparingly. The overwhelming majority of pilots were First or Second Lieutenants. A Base Commander had usually been an aviation leader before the war and was the only member to hold the rank of Major. The director of maintenance was called the Operations Officer. He was the base's second-in-command and usually a Captain. At most bases, saluting was not common and personnel only rarely stood in formation.

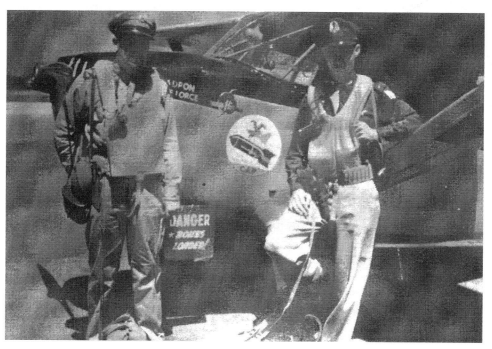

(6) BOMBS LOADED!
CP Base 3, Lantana Florida, CAP anti-sub pilots pose by
an armed Stinson Voyager. In the holster of the man on the right is
a signal flare gun.

(7) STINSON RELIANT
(CP Base 20, Bar Harbor, Maine)

Conditions at the 21 bases varied. Some took over oceanfront airports with full facilities. Others were primitive. At Coastal Patrol Base 9 in Louisiana, CAP fliers operated off a nearby highway and, for their headquarters, had only an abandoned hotel with no electricity. At CP Base 4 in Parksley, Virginia, pilots had to extend a runway by manual labor and convert a chicken coop into a barracks.

Everything was adapted, leveraged, unique, hybridized, creative, unusual, custom, special, begged, borrowed or "appropriated," but their effort endures as a hallmark of efficiency. The CAP also promoted donations and received gifts from states, towns, counties, civic groups and individuals. By the Coastal Patrol's end, CAP members had also contributed about a million dollars of their own money.

When a base reached ideal strength, it would have 78 personnel, including pilots, mechanics, guards and others, with much cross utilization of personnel. Their aircraft were cabin lightplanes, pulled from the ranks of American civil aviation, usually brought by their owners. They were capable of carrying two pilots and later, bombs or depth charges. Twenty five to thirty planes were authorized, preferably including an amphibious aircraft for ocean rescue.

CAP anti-sub planes were marked with a blue circle containing a white triangle, the symbol of Civil Defense. CAP's version of this symbol added a red, three-bladed propeller to its middle. This symbol was used for all aspects of the Civil Air Patrol except the external marking of anti-sub aircraft. For those CAP overwater planes, the red propeller was removed from the insignia for the same reason the U.S. Army Air Forces removed the red portion from their aircraft's insignia: its similarity to the "Rising Sun" marking on enemy Japanese aircraft operating in the Pacific.

CAP pilots may have started out to battle enemy submarines, but quickly realized that their peril of flying far out to sea, single engine, was a far greater danger. Engine maintenance was an absolute priority, and planes received early, precautionary overhauls. One base had a standing rule that the mechanic would fly as right-seat observer on the first overwater flight following engine work.

At CP Base Two in Rehoboth, Delaware, pilots said, "we fly by the grace of God and Smitty." Among the creative innovations of Captain Everett M. Smith were a quick release door system in case of ditching at sea, and the placement of several empty metal cans inside the fuselage. In the event of ditching, this flotation system kept the plane afloat with its tail feathers above water. This gave the surviving pilots something to hang onto and became a search marker visible for miles.

A few CAP fliers, when they arrived, were accustomed to airplanes with sophisticated instruments: radio direction finders, artificial horizon

(8) WACO CABIN BIPLANE
(CP Base 20, Bar Harbor, Maine)

indicators, and more. CAP patrol planes often had only minimum instruments, but those pilots flew out to sea anyway, learning to find their way by primitive, but skillful, pathfinding. They noted the numbers of offshore buoys, and learned to "read" the wave tops for wind direction. Many flew with radios so basic they had just a single channel.

With only these resources, the CAP patrolled in weather that grounded the regular military, whose planes had far superior equipment. CAP pilots could be caught under a ceiling as low as 100 feet, racing for home, due hard west into a headwind, radio useless, and their landing gear drenched with salt spray. However, the CAP could not fly effectively at night, when the submarines did their worst work.

Although dangerous, CAP's low search altitude was an advantage over the military. At only 500 feet, and flying slowly, they could scan the ocean's surface in far more detail, noting debris, floating wreckage, oil slicks, or possibly a raft full of survivors of a sinking. An actual "bogey," was, of course, a long, cigar-shaped discoloration under the waves or a periscope's feather wake on the surface.

Convoy escort was a mainstay of their work. As the CAP accompanied the merchant ships, sailors waved up from decks of freighters and tankers to show their appreciation.

CAP fliers had no parachutes, operating nowhere near high enough to use them. Besides inflatable vests, all they had at first for emergency flotation were automobile inner tubes, a situation which placed them in what one Base Commander considered a level of peril equivalent to armed troops on a battlefield. One-man, inflatable survival rafts arrived later, some not until March 1943.

(9) FAIRCHILD 24
(Warner radial engine) Note bomb.
(CP Base 2, Rehoboth, Delaware)

(10) FAIRCHILD 24 (Ranger inline engine)
(CP Base 5, Flagler Beach, Florida)

A typical mission day for a CAP Coastal Patrol pilot would be to wake up predawn in rented civilian housing, put on a uniform, then drive or catch a ride out to the base. There, he would receive a briefing, don a flotation vest or, in the winter, a larger, inflatable "zoot suit," and get into a Fairchild 24 or Stinson Voyager as a pilot or observer. Then he would take off into weather ranging from good to as low as a mile of visibility.

Two planes flew in formation for each other's safety. One aircraft was "lead," and the second plane, or "sister" ship, flew about 200 yards behind it and 200 yards to its right.

The reality of CAP's search and patrol was of flying long hours in monotony and tedium. The overwhelming majority of CAP's work was simply to confirm that all those square miles of empty ocean out there were indeed empty.

Another irony of their combat was that it took place in a part of the country that people had always flocked to for entertainment and relaxation. Summer tourists saw CAP and suspected their purpose but the CAP personnel couldn't discuss their mission.

Celebrities of the day who served at CAP Coastal Patrol bases included actress Mary Astor ("The Maltese Falcon"), actor Lee J. Cobb, film director Henry King and concert pianist José Iturbi.

As the months went by, the U.S. "arsenal of democracy" tooled up while the U-boat's presence dramatically reduced, thanks in large part to the CAP. After September 1942, there were no sinkings in U.S. waters, and in all of 1943, only three ships were lost.

(11) RYAN SCW (Sport Cabin/Warner engine)
(CP Base 6, St. Simon's Island, Georgia)

(12) STINSON VOYAGER (Note bomb).
This aircraft type is known by model designations including: 10, 10A, HW-75, 105, and others. (CP Base 21, Beaufort, North Carolina)

There was no patrol on the Pacific coast against Japanese "I-boat" submarines because of U.S. Naval presence there. Civil Air Patrol Coastal Patrol had lasted exactly 18 months. August 31, 1943 was the final day. During this entire period, overwater patrols of the regular military reportedly did not increase, and by one estimate, CAP flew two-thirds of all anti-sub patrol in U.S. waters.

———

WAS THIS THE MOST UNIQUE ARMED ACTION IN U.S. HISTORY?

This unusual force had prevailed. The CAP, operating with "one foot in and one foot out" of the military, flew civilian airplanes carrying bombs, far beyond safety limits, often with primitive equipment. Much of their unusual service had no precedent, and was invented as they went along. CAP was a "home guard," so rare in the modern American experience, and its personnel might be referred to as citizen-airmen.

CAP anti-sub pilots could also be considered as modern versions of American Revolutionary soldiers. Many CAP fliers brought their airplanes, like the colonists who arrived with their own muskets in 1776, and could be called "airborne minute men."

CAP's "civilian hands" story is also resonant to Britain's famed Dunkirk evacuation, wherein most of a huge retreating Allied army was saved in 1940 when hundreds of small private boats evacuated troops from waters too shallow for full-sized ships.

CAP was primarily effective because the U-boats would immediately flee upon seeing an airplane of any size, armed or not. But their presence in the air therefore affected huge, strategic global issues. Had the submarine's slaughter in U.S. waters continued, England could have fallen, greatly protracting the Allied force's method of Axis defeat.

CAP uniquely bridged civilian and military, but propelled by this unconventional energy, got a lot done. It all worked, in a vivid, modern example of plowshares doing the work of swords, and for a small fraction of what the regular military would have used. CAP is especially remarkable for getting so much done with so little an expenditure of funds.

(13) AN ARTIST'S IMPRESSION OF A CAP CIVILIAN GRUMMAN WIDGEON
amphibian dropping a depth charge on a German submarine.
(Illustration by Brian Hope)

CAP fliers may not have known the terms of today: citizen preparedness, homefront defense, homeland security, or anti-terrorism, but, in the modern machine age, they were achieving early versions of them.

Here are more of the fascinating facts of what might also be called "World War Two's Most Improbable Air Force:"

THE INCREDIBLE AND UNIQUE CIVIL AIR PATROL COASTAL PATROL OF WORLD WAR II

CIVIL AIR PATROL'S ALLEGED SUBMARINE KILL

"We're right over the periscope. Drop the depth charge!"

The destruction of an enemy German submarine would be the ultimate action of the CAP Coastal Patrol. There have been many reports that "the CAP got a couple of submarines," but especially that "the CAP destroyed a U-boat."

Here is the reported history: On July 17, 1942, Maj. Wynant Farr and Lt. Johnny Haggin *(Illustration #15)* were flying from Base One, Atlantic City, New Jersey in a civilian Grumman Widgeon amphibious airplane. *(Illustration #13)* Another CAP crew called in the sighting of an enemy U-boat cruising below periscope depth. Farr and Haggin hastened to the scene and spotted the distinctive underwater silhouette, too low for their depth charge's setting. *(Illustration #14)* They reportedly followed the submarine for three hours, and were at their fuel limit when the U-boat reportedly ascended almost to periscope depth. They dropped their depth charge and later reported that the submarine's bow breached the surface. Debris was reportedly found by the U.S. Navy.

This incident became regarded as a CAP submarine kill, and has become a continuous source of validation and inspiration for Civil Air Patrol anti-sub. However, in all of anti-submarine warfare (ASW), results are uncertain. Pending a full investigation of both United States and

German naval records, this incident should be regarded as a reported kill, and not a verified one.

A rumored second submarine kill by CAP has never been reliably verified or documented.

(14) CAP GRUMMAN WIDGEON
Note nose of wing-mounted depth charge at lower left.

(15) MAJOR WYNANT C. FARR and **CAPT. JOHNNY HAGGIN**

"SCARE THE SUB DOWN"

"The sub's about to spot that freighter. Dive down and fly right at its periscope."

In the early months of the war, before they became armed, CAP pilots, upon spotting an invading U-boat at periscope depth or below, attempted to track the enemy's progress while calling for an armed attack by the regular U.S. military. But on occasion, they realized the submarine was about to discover a "target" of its own, usually a freighter or a tanker. Then, the unarmed CAP aircraft would descend to just a few feet above the waves and fly directly into the periscope's line of vision. In every case, the U-boat immediately submerged. Although no official credit could be given, those CAP crews could take satisfaction that they may have saved an Allied merchant ship and the lives of its crewmen.

(16) INSTALLING A BOMB UNDERNEATH THE BELLY OF A RYAN SCW.
(CP Base 4, Parksley, Virginia)

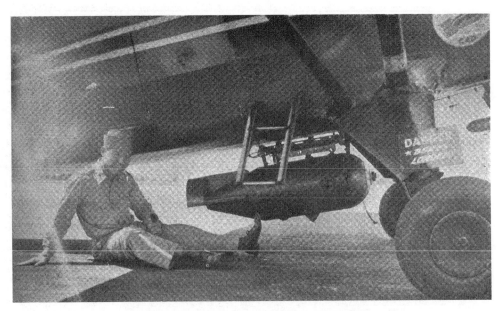

(17) ZACK MOSLEY, CAP ANTI-SUB PILOT
and nationally syndicated cartoonist of "Smilin' Jack," gestures to a 325 depth charge
underneath a Stinson Reliant. For ground clearance, a CAP mechanic
had removed one of its four fins – with a hacksaw!
(CP Base 3, Lantana, Florida)

HOW THE CAP COASTAL PATROL BECAME ARMED

"I don't care if they have to throw 'em out the window!"

Despite the severity of the enemy submarine menace, the regular U.S. military was reluctant to give munitions to civilians. The extreme order to arm the CAP was a single, impassioned decision by one individual exercising command decision.

It was during March and April of 1942, the earliest months of CAP Coastal Patrol's service, that they had most of their encounters with enemy U-boats. But during this time period the CAP was not armed.

In April, the crew of an unarmed CAP aircraft flying from Coastal Patrol Base Three, Lantana, Florida, spotted a surfaced enemy submarine near the mouth of the Banana River. The U-boat immediately attempted to escape, but embedded its nose in a mudbank or sandbar and stuck there. The sub ran its propellers at full power, furiously attempting to flee. CAP pilots Thomas Manning and M.E. "Doc" Rinker circled the stranded enemy craft for almost 45 minutes, radioing frantically for the U.S. regular military. By the time a Navy bomber arrived, the submarine had broken free.

This incident made General Henry H. "Hap" Arnold, Commanding General of the U.S. Army Air Forces, order that the Civil Air Patrol be armed. He reportedly said, "Give the CAP bombs. I don't care if they have to throw 'em out the window!"

Bombs and their racks were military hardware, but the method of attaching them to each civilian CAP aircraft was different. Shackles were bolted onto the lower steel tubes inside fabric-covered aircraft, and holes were drilled in the bellies of sheet metal aircraft *(Illustration #16)* to hold racks for weapons ranging from 100 pound bombs up to 325 pound depth charges. *(Illustration #17)*

(18) SIKORSKY S-39 RESCUE AMPHIBIAN
(CP Base 2, Rehoboth, Delaware)

TOP RIGHT
(19) RESCUE of **LT. HENRY CROSS** by **MAJOR HUGH SHARP** and
LT. "EDDIE" EDWARDS (Illustration by Brian Hope)

(20) TWO AIR MEDALS FOR CAP VALOR FROM PRESIDENT ROOSEVELT.
(National Archives)

(19)

TWO CAP HEROES MEET THE PRESIDENT OF THE UNITED STATES

"Plane down!"

The CAP Coastal Patrol featured countless episodes of bravery but one incident is regarded as a standout.

On July 21, 1942, a CAP crew flying from Coastal Patrol Base Two, Rehoboth, Delaware, radioed an emergency call. Their "sister" ship had undergone an engine failure and ditched into the ocean.

Base Commander Major Hugh Sharp, Jr. and Lt. Edmond "Eddie" Edwards took off in the Base's Sikorsky amphibian. *(Illustration #18)* This aircraft, kept for rescue, was originally built for the light inland waters of a lake or river but now roared out over the sea. They set down in high ocean swells, damaging the left outboard wing-float. As Sharp taxied, Edwards picked up the injured pilot, Lt. Henry Cross *(Illustration #19),* but they could not find the other crewmember, Lt. Charles Shelfus.

Unable to take off, they taxied through the sea. The damaged float filled with water and dipped down into the swells. Edwards crawled out to the right side and sat on the undamaged float to balance the aircraft as Sharp taxied through the ocean waves. During the ordeal, Edwards was, from time to time, almost completely immersed in sea water. A Coast Guard boat met them near nightfall and towed them to Chincoteague, Virginia, where they arrived early the following morning.

Edwards's hands were cramped, almost numb, from grasping the float's struts. Cross recovered and in February 1943, Sharp and Edwards were personally awarded the Air Medal, in the Oval Office of the White House, by President Franklin D. Roosevelt. *(Illustration #20)*

This Sikorsky S-39 aircraft is now on display at the New England Air Museum, Windsor Locks, Connecticut.

TOP RIGHT
(21) AIRBORNE "DAVID" AGAINST INVADING "GOLIATH."
Artist's impression of an armed CAP Stinson Voyager about to attack a German U-boat.
(Illustration by Brian Hope)

(21)

FLYING AGAINST AN ENEMY OVER FIVE HUNDRED TIMES YOUR OWN SIZE

"I don't care how big it is. Let's go!"

There are many stories in folklore and military history of a hero prevailing over an antagonist many times his or her own size. CAP Coastal Patrol provides an especially strong example of this.

Illustration #21 depicts a CAP Stinson Voyager aircraft with a 100 lb. bomb about to attack a U-boat. There is no known instance of an armed Civil Air Patrol aircraft directly attacking a surfaced submarine. But if a Voyager had done so, the image is especially pleasing: the small aircraft's gross weight is 1680 pounds, and a German Type Seven U-boat weighed at least 500 tons. The CAP aircraft is therefore attacking an enemy, by weight, over 500 times its own size.

LIVE AT HOME AND GO TO WAR

"I'm off to war, honey. I'll be back by suppertime."

Some CAP Coastal Patrol members lived in their own homes while serving at a nearby anti-sub base. On a patrol day, they might rise early at home, put on their uniform, and drive in the pre-dawn darkness to the Base. There, they would receive a briefing, and then fly an armed airplane out over the ocean, possibly to engage in armed warfare with an enemy of the United States. They could later return to supper with their families. This is a situation the United States fighting man, up to this time, had seldom, if ever, seen since the American Revolution.

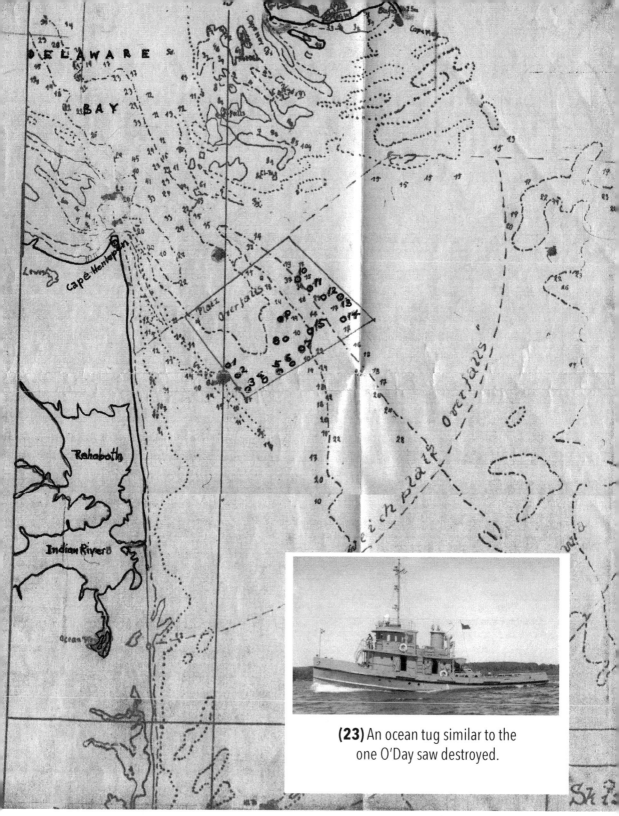

(23) An ocean tug similar to the
one O'Day saw destroyed.

(24) MAP OF 15 MINES laid by U-373 offshore from Rehoboth Beach
at night, June 11, 1942. (Shore feature names in English added post-war).
(Gift to author from Fred Geils, radar operator on the U-373)

CAP DIRECT EYEWITNESSES TO WARFARE

(Boom!) "What happened to the tugboat?"

Civil Air Patrol anti-sub crews often responded in the aftermath of a sinking, to search for survivors or to look for the attacking submarine. But in at least one case, CAP personnel were direct eyewitnesses to a sinking caused by enemy action.

In the dark, early morning hours of June 11, 1942, the German submarine U-373, operating about six miles off Rehoboth Beach, Delaware, laid 15 mines to destroy Allied ships. On either June 11th or 12th, CAP Base Two pilot Lt. Roland "Tom" O'Day *(Illustration #22)* was flying on patrol over this area with an unknown observer. He noted an American oceangoing tugboat, an "ocean tug." *(Illustration #23)* Moving his eyes left and right in observation "sweeps," O'Day thought he heard something, turned back towards the ocean tug, and saw a geyser of water settling back down to the ocean. The ocean tug and its crew had been instantly obliterated with the loss of all hands. After an intense search produced no submarine sighting, U.S. authorities suspected a mine laid by a U-boat at night. U.S. minesweeper ships located, and detonated, the remainder of the mines *(Illustration #24)* and shipping resumed safely. But, by this incident, civilian-airmen of the Civil Air Patrol were direct eyewitnesses to enemy action, in daylight, and within sight of the American homeland coast.

(22) LT. ROLAND "TOM" O'DAY

(also see "Enemies No More," Illustration #82)

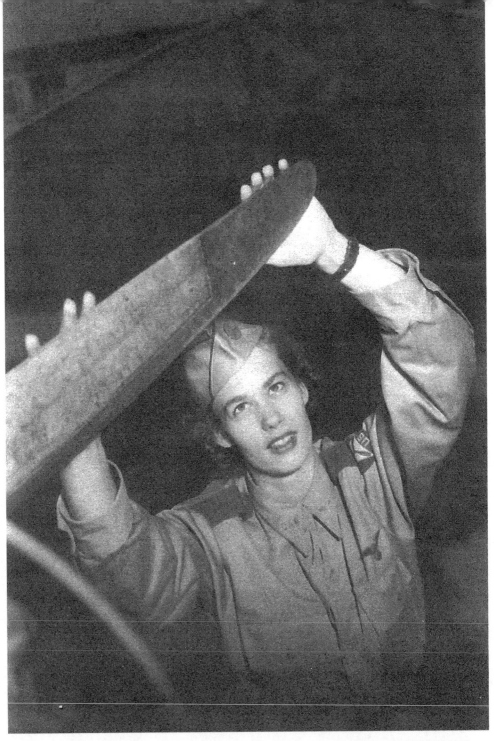

(25) WOMEN SERVED IN ALMOST ALL OF CAP'S WORLD WAR TWO DUTIES.

WOMEN OF THE CAP
COASTAL PATROL

Women were part of the Civil Air Patrol from the start and participated in almost all CAP duties. *(Illustration #25)* Their exclusion from flying Coastal Patrol was not based on any factor of skill or ability but of the fear of a woman pilot ditching into the ocean and encountering a German submarine crew.

Women flew search, rescue and courier missions. They led many CAP squadrons and some of CAP's state organizations, called "wings."

Women assisted at all Coastal Patrol bases. Married and single women served as base radio operators and performed administrative and other duties. *(Illustration #26)* Many were wives of CAP fliers or other personnel. Some pilots' wives lived near a Base, traveling to be with their husbands. Some wives took factory or other jobs back at home and supported themselves and their children, enabling their husbands to fly CAP anti-sub.

(26) WOMAN RADIO OPERATOR AT BASE 17 (SGT. SHAFFER)
(CP Base 17, Suffolk, New York)

CAP PERSONNEL WERE NOT BOUND TO STAY

"I'm sorry, Major, but my family needs me back at home."

Civil Air Patrol personnel, even at an armed anti-sub Base, were not bound to stay there. Unlike the regular military, a CAP Base Commander had no official power over his personnel. There are no reported incidents of trouble regarding this factor. Occasionally, pilots or other staff members informed their Base Commander, usually with regret, that they had to leave because of family or business obligations. In the first months of Coastal Patrol, some personnel may have been compelled to leave because funds had not arrived to pay them.

(27) AUTOMOBILE TIRE INNER TUBE
For many months, before receiving inflatable rafts, all that CAP pilots had in the event of ditching were their flotation vests and these tubes.

TOP RIGHT
(28) A BASE TWO PILOT DEMONSTRATES INFLATABLE SURVIVAL RAFT.
(CP Base 2, Rehoboth, Delaware)

(28)

THE CLUB NOBODY WANTED TO JOIN
THE "DUCK CLUB"

"Pilot down!"

CAP pilots may have flown out to sea ready to do battle with a German submarine, but quickly realized that flying single-engine overwater was their far greater danger.

As the Coastal Patrol started, all pilots had for flotation were inflatable vests and automobile inner tubes. *(Illustration #27)* CP Base 4 Commander Maj. Isaac Burnham later commented that this put his men in a level of peril equivalent to a shooting war on a battlefield. One-man inflatable rafts arrived later, some as late as the winter of 1943. *(Illustration #28)*

Many CAP Coastal Patrol pilots underwent engine failures which resulted in a forced ditching into the sea. Those who survived became members of the "Duck Club," which totaled 112 members.

The Duck Club is similar to aviation's Caterpillar Club, an organization made up only of pilots who have involuntarily parachuted ("taken to the silk") from a stricken aircraft. *(Also see Illustrations #29, #30)*

(29) FUSELAGE OF A WACO CABIN BIPLANE
recovered after the CAP aircraft ditched. The wrinkled fabric shows the force of impact.
Both pilots survived. (CP Base 2, Rehoboth, Delaware)

(30) "DUCK CLUB" MEMBERS.
Each of these Rehoboth, Delaware CP Base 2 pilots survived a ditching at sea:
Harvey P. Cannon, Thomas Sanschagrin, Warren O. Smith, Logan Grier,
John W. Chew, Jr., Walter Fullerton. Not pictured: Henry Cross

THE UNIQUE ECONOMICS
OF CAP COASTAL PATROL

"You've got to help us. Our patrol is saving your tankers!"

As the Coastal Patrol began in the early months of 1942, CAP's funding channels were not fully set up, forcing some bases to near comic scarcity. The personnel of New Jersey's Base One, about to be evicted from their housing, went directly to area oil companies in desperation. They argued that their patrol helped save the companies' tankers and boosted the morale of their crews. That afternoon, the cash tills of some Atlantic City gas stations were emptied to help the Base.

In Beaumont, Texas, CP Base 10 reportedly supplemented its budget -- in multiple levels of irony -- by selling bales of rubber that washed ashore from freighters torpedoed in the Gulf of Mexico by the very enemies they wished to fight!

Funding finally came through, but even after the economic situation had stabilized, CAP Coastal Patrol bases operated with a continuous commercial presence, so rare for armed actions. *(Illustration #31)* Instead of salaries, CAP anti-sub personnel received per diem ("by the day") payments, and could be considered to have functioned as contractors. From these funds, they paid for their own housing, food, clothing and personal equipment. The following list of these allotments underscores the unique, and even ironic, economic nature of the CAP Coastal Patrol: • Base Commander: $10/day • Pilots, operations and assistant operations officers, pilot-observers, engineering and intelligence operators, flight surgeons: $8/day • Non-pilot observers, assistant engineering and intelligence officers, radio operators, airdrome officer, mechanics, and radio mechanics: $7/day • Administrative section head: $6/day • Other ground personnel, apprentice mechanics, plotting board operators, clerk-typists, linemen, and guards: $5/day • Personnel were allowed one paid day off per week. Aircraft owners were usually also pilots and were compensated by the hour for the use of their airplanes. Here is a sample of an hourly-usage payment structure for airplanes of the 90-120 HP category • Operations and Maintenance: $4.40 • Depreciation: $3.50 • Insurance: $2.75 • When equipped with a bomb rack, aircraft owners received an additional $6.75 per hour for added insurance cost. These allotments for depreciation and insurance can be regarded as very unique. *(See next page.)*

There was, however, no room for profiteers. One CAP Coastal Patrol aircraft pilot/owner calculated that his compensations, after expenses, brought him a monthly "salary" of less than ten dollars.

(31) AN ADMINISTRATIVE STAFF AT EACH BASE KEPT FULL BOOKKEEPING
and other records. (CP Base 2, Rehoboth, Delaware)

CAP INSURANCE POLICIES
FOR ARMED ACTIONS

". . . nor does it cover . . . injury sustained by being shot at or bombed by any person whatsoever or . . . participation by the Insured in actual hostilities, or . . . by the act of any enemy of the United States."

Civil Air Patrol Coastal Patrol personnel purchased medical insurance policies provided on a group basis by the CAP. Aircraft owners had a separate policy to insure their airplanes. Commercial insurance policies for armed actions by civilians on behalf of the United States are extremely unusual documents. The medical policies included an especially ironic touch: if CAP personnel encountered a submarine, they were *not* covered for injury from direct enemy fire.

(32) TO THE RIGHT OF THE WACO AIRCRAFT'S PROPELLER:
husband and wife Muriel and Rudie Chalow. (CP Base 1, Atlantic City, New Jersey)

HUSBANDS AND WIVES SERVED AT THE SAME CAP ARMED BASE

"Your husband is in the ocean!"

Some husbands and wives served together at CAP anti-sub bases. During this era of World War II, this may be the only time this had happened in a U.S. armed action since the American Revolution or the Civil War. The wife of a CAP pilot or other specialist often served as a radio operator or on the Base's administrative staff.

Coastal Patrol Base One, Atlantic City, New Jersey was the site of an especially dramatic incident involving spouses. Muriel Chalow, a woman radio operator who had just left her station for lunch, was suddenly informed that her husband, Rudie, had just ditched into winter ocean waters following an engine failure. Fortunately, he had set down next to a Coast Guard boat and he and his fellow crewman were rescued. *(Illustration #32)*

NO OFFICIAL DEFERMENT
FROM DRAFT

"I'm sorry, Major, but I must leave. I've been drafted."

All of CAP's World War Two services, including the armed Coastal Patrol, provided no official deferment from a man being drafted into the regular U.S. military. Many CAP pilots were already sworn into the regular military but waiting to be called up. Local draft boards, on a case-by-case basis, might have allowed temporary deferments for CAP anti-sub personnel. But it was also possible for a CAP Coastal Patrol Base to lose a trained anti-sub pilot or other specialist to boot camp in the regular military.

CAP OPERATED UNDER THE JURISDICTION OF THE CIVIL AERONAUTICS ADMINISTRATION

All services of the Civil Air Patrol, including the armed Coastal Patrol, operated under the jurisdiction of the U.S. governmental agency that regulated civilian flying, the Civil Aeronautics Administration. The CAA was the forerunner of today's Federal Aviation Administration, or FAA.

CAP anti-sub pilots carried pilot's licenses and medical cards. They recorded CAP flights in their civilian pilot logbooks. Full CAA maintenance records were kept for all CAP aircraft. Some of their civilian airframe logbooks included entries to install bomb racks, including weight and balance forms, as if the aircraft were flying in routine domestic activity.

Checkrides for pilot competence could theoretically be demanded by CAA officials. It was also possible for a CAA official to "ground" a CAP pilot or airplane for an infraction of regulations. If incidents like this happened at all, they were very rare.

**(33) CAPT. JOSEPH N. HETTEL, BY THE FRONT OF HIS
BASE'S SIKORSKY S-39 RESCUE AMPHIBIAN.**
On Sept. 15, 1942, Hettel, flying a Waco cabin biplane, became one of 82 CAP
anti-sub pilots to drop a bomb on a target believed to be an enemy submarine.
His logbook entry: "Sighted Nazi sub – Bombed same." (CP Base 17, Suffolk, New York)

THIS CAMPAIGN WAS, TECHNICALLY, A TWO-WAY SHOOTING WAR

"Turn around fast. That sub's shooting at us!"

Although the overwhelming value of CAP's anti-sub patrol was as a deterrent force, CAP pilots dropped bombs or depth charges on targets believed to be submarines 82 times. *(Illustration #33)* There is no conclusive knowledge of the outcome of any of these actions. The possibility exists that the CAP actually destroyed an enemy submarine. In all of anti-submarine warfare (ASW), results are notoriously uncertain. But in every one of these incidents, live weapons were discharged in war action, and can be considered to be "shots fired in anger."

The CAP Coastal Patrol drew fire in at least one incident. Base Five pilots, flying routine daytime patrol from Flagler Beach, Florida, encountered an enemy submarine on the ocean surface. The U-boat was probably charging its batteries, had its anti-aircraft guns ready, and fired shots. The CAP airplane immediately turned away, escaping without damage. (Source: *From Maine To Mexico* (Keefer), p. 119). It is not recorded whether this CAP aircraft was armed at the time. There may have been other such incidents.

In histories of armed conflict, the words "shots were traded" has been used to establish a belligerent tone, a physical level of conflict, or to indicate that a war was underway. Of course, a campaign in which each side immediately fled upon sight of, or shots fired by, the other can hardly be compared to real engagements of the regular military, but the CAP Coastal Patrol's campaign against invading German U-boats can be technically called a "two-way shooting war."

AN ALBUM OF PHOTOGRAPHS OF CIVIL AIR PATROL COASTAL PATROL

(PAGES 47-67)
(Illustrations #35-#66)

(35) A CAP "RAFT SAVE"
The Civil Air Patrol Coastal Patrol is credited with finding 363
survivors in the ocean water. Upon rescue, many reported that large
airplanes of the regular military had flown over them at high altitude,
but that they were found and saved by the "low and slow" patrol
work of the CAP. (CP Base 3, Lantana, Florida)

(36) OFFICERS OF CP BASE 17,
Suffolk, Long Island, New York,
pose with an empty bomb adorned with their Base's insignia.

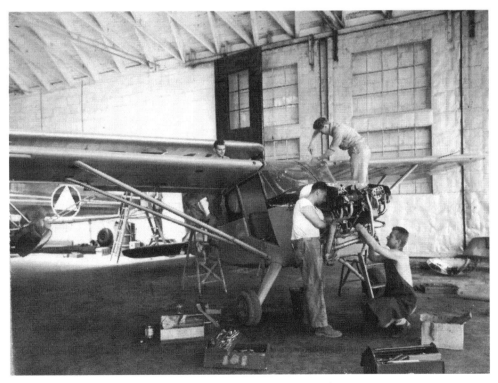

(34) ENGINE MAINTENANCE for CAP anti-sub aircraft was an absolute priority.
Early, precautionary overhauls were done and airframes were given
extreme ongoing care. (CP Base 17, Suffolk, New York)

(37) "LEMME AT 'EM!"
– this CAP pilot seems to be saying, arm propped on the wing float of a Sikorsky S-39 rescue amphibian.
But the handgun in his holster was used for guard duty at the base.
(CP Base 17, Suffolk, New York)

(38) BRIEFING ROOM AT BASE 17, SUFFOLK, LONG ISLAND, NEW YORK.
The pilot at the far right has a large knife in a sheath on his belt. In the event of ditching, this was to knock out his airplane's plastic windows to help exit the aircraft.

(39) CLASSROOM AT CP BASE 17, SUFFOLK, LONG ISLAND, NEW YORK.
Navigation and meteorology were prime courses.

(40) CAP LINE CREW MEMBERS PREPARE A WACO CABIN BIPLANE.
This gas truck would have been 10-15
years old at the time. (CP Base 2, Rehoboth, Delaware)

(41) PILOT AND OBSERVER PREPARE TO FLY A STINSON VOYAGER ON PATROL.
(CP Base 20, Bar Harbor, Maine)

(42) POSED PICTURE OF A CAP PILOT HAND-PROPPING A STINSON VOYAGER.
Virtually all CAP anti-sub aircraft – including Stinson Voyagers –
were equipped with electric starters. (CP Base 20, Bar Harbor, Maine)

(43) LONG AND THOROUGH PRE-FLIGHT INSPECTIONS
were done before flying overwater patrols. (CP Base 20, Bar Harbor, Maine)

(44) STINSON VOYAGER LANDING
at CP Base 20, Bar Harbor, Maine.

(45) HANGAR OF CAP ANTI-SUB PLANES AT CP BASE 17, SUFFOLK, LONG ISLAND, NEW YORK.
Note the Civil Defense symbol on top left wing of aircraft in right foreground has been painted in reverse orientation.

(46) AGGRESSIVE ENGINE MAINTENANCE
at CP Base 17, Suffolk, New York.

(47) RECOVERING A FABRIC WING AT CP BASE 17, SUFFOLK, NEW YORK.
Such involved airframe maintenance would be performed only when time permitted,
or when no other airworthy aircraft parts were available.

(48) VIEW FROM THE RUNWAY AT CP BASE 2,
Rehoboth, Delaware, on a busy patrol day.

(49) A CAP ANTI-SUB BASE
often took over what had been a seaside town's municipal airport before the war.
(CP Base 2, Rehoboth, Delaware)

(50) A CIVIL AIR PATROL SEAPLANE BASE.

CP Base 2, Rehoboth, Delaware, maintained this facility for a few months on Rehoboth Bay. There was some speculation that aircraft on floats would be safer to operate over the ocean. They could alight on the water in the event of engine trouble or even possibly to aid those in distress on the sea. There is no recorded instance of a CAP floatplane landing on the ocean.

**(51) LT. ARTHUR "TOM" WORTH STANDING
ON THE FLOAT OF A FAIRCHILD 24 SEAPLANE.**
(CP Base 2, Rehoboth, Delaware)

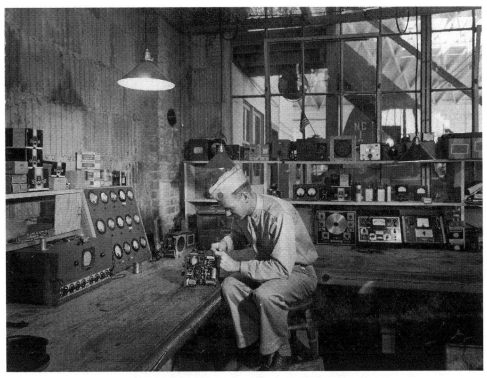

**(52) RADIO MAINTENANCE AT CP BASE 17,
SUFFOLK, LONG ISLAND, NEW YORK.**
Many CAP anti-sub bases had no such deluxe communications.

(53) MEMBERS OF CP BASE 17, SUFFOLK, LONG ISLAND, NEW YORK
march in formation at their patrol's conclusion. At most CAP anti-sub bases, saluting
was not common, and personnel only occasionally stood in formation.

(54) A CIVIL AIR PATROL CONTROL TOWER
The operator is flashing light-gun signals
to aircraft on the runway and taxiway below.
(CP Base 17, Suffolk, New York)

SUBMARINE BELOW---
FLASHES THE CIVIL AIR PATROL PLANE

The indistinct shadow beneath the water means little to the untrained eye—but, the C. A. P. Pilot and his Observer instantly recognize the outline of a lurking enemy submarine preparing for destruction and death. The Pilot's depth charge is soon on its way—the location radioed to the Army, Navy and Coast Guard. The destruction of the raider is imminent.

Former commercial and pleasure fliers who volunteered their services and their airplanes, the men of the Civil Air Patrol have been risking their lives daily since Pearl Harbor in the grim, relentless search for Axis submarines off our shores. Many ships have been saved from torpedoing—many already-shipwrecked seamen rescued—thanks to their ceaseless patrol. To them belongs no small share of the credit for driving the enemy undersea raiders away from our coasts.

We salute them for the courage, ability and self-sacrifice with which they do their job—and we are proud that many of the planes in which they perform this service to the Nation are Jacobs-powered.

JACOBS *Engines* **AIRCRAFT**
POTTSTOWN • PENNSYLVANIA   U S A

(55) U.S. MANUFACTURERS WERE QUICK TO PUBLICIZE THE USEFULNESS OF THEIR WAR-RELATED PRODUCTS.

CAP personnel had access to stateside publications and were among the few armed troops to see their own war actions depicted in the commercial media. Here, a cabin Waco biplane - using a Jacobs engine - is depicted on CAP Coastal Patrol.

(56) BRAVE CAP ANTI-SUB PILOTS OFTEN FLEW OVERWATER WITH MINIMAL RADIO EQUIPMENT, SUCH AS SETS WITH ONLY ONE CHANNEL.

Some aviation radio manufacturers, in their magazine advertisements, depicted CAP anti-sub pilots as using their more sophisticated sets. These ads were read at Coastal Patrol bases, and we can only speculate on the reaction to them by those CAP crews, flying daily in overwater danger, who did not have, or couldn't afford, such luxurious equipment.

(57) (58) TO START AIRCRAFT ENGINES IN THE WINTER,
Captain Everett M. Smith built this motor driven external starter, mounted on a truck
bed. The truck was driven to the front of the airplane, a second motor on the truck bed
was started, and a metal spindle interlocked with a fitting on the aircraft's prop hub,
force-turning it. The spindle automatically retracted when the aircraft engine "caught."
(CP Base 2, Rehoboth, Delaware)

**(59) (60) RARE PHOTOS OF CAP ADULT MEMBERS
DOING PHYSICAL TRAINING.**
(Note maintenance hangar in background)
(CP Base 2, Rehoboth, Delaware)

(61) LUNCH COUNTER
at CP Base 17, Suffolk, New York

(62) FAMILY AND FRIENDS could visit CAP anti-sub personnel, and were usually
allowed on base premises. Pilots depicted: Henry "Ed" Phipps
and Glen Cook. (CP Base 2, Rehoboth, Delaware)

(63) A FEW BASES ORGANIZED A BASEBALL TEAM,
often to play against personnel of the regular military.
(CP Base 17, Suffolk, New York)

(64) IMPROMPTU HUMOR
at the canteen of CP Base 3, Lantana, Florida.

This poem was written by Lt. Elbert C. Isom, a pilot in CAP Coastal Patrol Base 10 (Beaumont, Texas). It described how CAP's anti-sub patrol might have been perceived by captains and crews of the ships they protected:

When the cold grey dawn is breaking,
And the wolf pack hovers nigh;
When the skipper scans the ocean,
With a grim and worried eye,

Then a distant sound grows louder,
And brings comfort to his soul;
For he knows his ship is covered,
By the Civil Air Patrol.

(66) CP BASE TWO, REHOBOTH, DELAWARE AT PEAK STRENGTH (MARCH 1943).

(67) A MAJOR SHOW OF CAP FORCE
in Lansing, Michigan during WWII.

(68) A CAP GROUP
(location unknown) poses by a Rearwin aircraft.

CIVIL AIR PATROL'S OTHER WORLD WAR II SERVICES IN ALL 48 STATES

Approximately 1700 CAP personnel participated in its Coastal Patrol, but tens of thousands performed other Civil Air Patrol duties throughout America. The CAP put much of U.S. civil aviation into uniform and performed support services for the U.S. Office of Civilian Defense and later, as the Auxiliary of the Army Air Forces. *(Illustration #67)*

During World War Two, the Civil Air Patrol mobilized into 48 state organizations, called "wings." Each wing was comprised of many squadrons. In addition to Coastal Patrol, CAP performed: Aircraft Search, Courier Service, Pipeline Surveillance, Tow Target, Forest Patrol, Power Line Patrol, and a Southern Liaison Patrol along the United States/ Mexican border to guard against the possibility of infiltrating spies or other incursions. CAP's cadet program began in October 1942 and included male and female cadets from the beginning.

The Coastal Patrol established 90 horsepower, usually of the Stinson Voyager, as an aircraft's minimum for overwater operations. But all of CAP's other services used aircraft of many sizes, especially utilizing lower-horsepower lightplanes such as Piper Cub, Aeronca, Taylorcraft, Luscombe, Porterfield, Rearwin *(Illustration #68)*, Culver, and others. CAP's inland services also utilized a very few open cockpit aircraft types.

(69) A STINSON OF CAP TOW TARGET SQUADRON 22 BEGINNING TO DEPLOY ITS TARGET SLEEVE.
The target would be reeled out to approximately 1200 feet behind the towing aircraft before being fired upon.

THE HAZARDS OF
TOW-TARGET DUTY

Of all CAP's World War Two services, "Tow Target" duty may have been the most dramatic of all.

Following de-activation of the Coastal Patrol in 1943, several former anti-sub Bases were converted to Tow Target Squadrons and transferred to other locations. They were no longer armed, but pulled target sleeves behind their CAP aircraft for practice shots of live gunnery by ground installations or aircraft of the regular military. *(Illustration #69)*

When live gunnery shots came closer to their towing aircraft than to the target sleeve, CAP pilots would humorously speculate that the gun crews might be saying, "What was that long white sleeve so far behind the target we were shooting at?"

But for two pilots of CAP Tow Target Squadron 22, these words almost assumed a very grim reality. *(Illustrations #70, #71)*

(70) THIS PHOTO SHOWS THE EXTREME HAZARDS OF TOW TARGET DUTY.
In this instance, the live practice shots (firing source unknown) missed the target
sleeve, instead almost directly hitting this CAP Waco cabin biplane towing it.
Note the aircraft's torn, shredded, and missing fabric.

(71) TOW TARGET PILOT
Lt. Norman Rehrig humorously poses with
a stethoscope to "examine" his co-pilot, believed to be
Lt. Adolph Backstrom, following the ordeal. (Tow Target Squadron 22)

(72) U.S. COAST GUARD AUXILIARY SAILBOATS.

CAP COASTAL PATROL'S SIMILARITY TO THE U.S. COAST GUARD AUXILIARY OF WORLD WAR II

The Civil Air Patrol Coastal Patrol is especially resonant with a seagoing counterpart, the U.S. Coast Guard Auxiliary. The CGA used converted yachts, sailboats, and other craft to perform many support duties, including ocean patrol for invading U-boats. Their strategy, if they saw an enemy submarine, was to radio for an armed boat, ship or airplane of the regular U.S. military. A CGA boat's armament might include a surplus World War One machine gun, mounted on its deck. This was not to directly challenge an enemy submarine but to keep order on the water, possibly if encountering a surrendering enemy crew who had been forced to abandon their U-boat. The CGA also carried five-pound explosive charges in small metal buckets. Upon seeing the periscope of a sub about to discover an Allied merchant ship, the CGA crew would fling these charges off their own stern to confuse the submarine's sonar operator and make the U-boat flee. There is one incident, passed down as oral history, in which a CGA sailboat *(Illustration #72)* spotted a surfaced U-boat off Long Island, New York, at night. The CGA charged from long distance, under both auxiliary engine and sail power, its machine gun firing. The German submarine, which could have easily destroyed the small craft with its deck gun, instead elected to submerge and leave.

(73) LT. DELMONT "DEL" GARRETT (pictured) died with Lt. Paul D. Towne, on March 19, 1943, following a ditching into the ocean while flying anti-sub patrol from Base 2, Rehoboth, Delaware.

THE 26 CIVIL AIR PATROL COASTAL PATROL PILOTS WHO LOST THEIR LIVES

Of the several hundred pilots who flew with CAP Coastal Patrol, 26 lost their lives, most in the aftermath of a forced ditching into the sea.

Pictured in *Illustration #73* is Base Two pilot 1st Lt. Delmont ("Del") B. Garrett, who died with 1st Lt. Paul Towne on March 19, 1943, following an engine failure/forced ditching into the sea.

**These are the 26 Coastal Patrol pilots
who lost their lives, including name,
base number and location, and date of death:**

1st Lt. C. W. Andrews (Base 14, Panama City, Florida), October 30, 1942 -- **1st Lt. Ben Berger** (Base 1, Atlantic City, New Jersey), April 25, 1943 -- **1st Lt. Curtis P. Black** (Base 14, Panama City, Florida), January 4, 1943 -- **1st Lt. Welles L. Bishop** (Base 20, Bar Harbor, Maine), February 2, 1943 -- **1st Lt. Guy T. Cherry, Jr.** (Base 21, Beaufort, North Carolina), November 16, 1942 -- **1st Lt. Frank M. Cook** (Base 16, Manteo, North Carolina), December 21, 1942 -- **1st Lt. Julian L. Cooper** (Base 16, Manteo, North Carolina), December 21, 1942 -- **2nd Lt. Martin E. Coughlin** (Base 11, Pascagoula, Mississippi), February 26, 1943 -- **1st Lt. Paul W. Davis** (Base 11, Pascagoula, Mississippi), February 26, 1943 -- **1st Lt. John H. Dean** (Base 10, Beaumont, Texas), November 16, 1942 -- **2nd Lt. Donald C. Ferner** (Base 14, Panama City, Florida), April 3, 1943 -- **1st Lt. Delmont B. Garrett** (Base 2,

Rehoboth, Delaware), March 19, 1943 -- **1st Lt. William B. Hites** (Base 20, Bar Harbor, Maine), February 2, 1943 -- **2nd Lt. D.L. King** (Base 8, Charleston, South Carolina), February 9, 1943 -- **1st Lt. Alfred H. Koym** (Base 10, Beaumont, Texas), November 11, 1942 -- **Capt. H.L. Lindquist** (Base 21, Beaufort, North Carolina), June 27, 1943 -- **1st Lt. L. E. Milkey** (Base 14, Panama City, Florida), October 30, 1942 -- **1st Lt. Gerald G. Owen** (Base 14, Panama City, Florida), April 3, 1943 -- **2nd Lt. C.L. Rawls** (Base 8, Charleston, South Carolina), February 9, 1943 -- **1st Lt. Charles Shelfus** (Base 2, Rehoboth, Delaware), July 21, 1942 -- **1st Lt. H. O. Swift** (Base 2, Rehoboth, Delaware), March 6, 1943 -- **1st Lt. James C. Taylor** (Base 10, Beaumont, Texas), November 11, 1942 -- **1st Lt. Paul D. Towne** (Base 2, Rehoboth, Delaware), March 19, 1943 -- **1st Lt. Alvie T. Vaughen** (Base 14, Panama City, Florida), January 4, 1943 -- **1st Lt. Robert D. Ward** (Base 10, Beaumont, Texas), November 16, 1942 -- **Flight Officer D. S. Williams** (Base 21, Beaufort, North Carolina), June 27, 1943.

(74) OFTEN THE BODY OF A LOST CAP FLIER WAS NOT RECOVERED.
As an expression of their grief, Coastal Patrol pilots would drop floral wreaths onto the
ocean in memory of a lost comrade. Base Two at Rehoboth, Delaware,
among the hardest hit of the 21 Coastal Patrol bases, lost four men.
(Note: for winter flying, the pilots are wearing large, inflatable "zoot" suits.)
(Also see Illustration #79, Rehoboth memorial stone).

(75) 1948 AIR MEDAL CEREMONY
at the Rehoboth, Delaware airport.

(76) FORMER BASE 2 COMMANDER, HUGH SHARP, JR.
speaks at 1948 Air Medal ceremony.

CAP COASTAL PATROL VETERANS AFTER THE WAR

By the summer of 1943, the regular U.S. military was able to fully take over America's coastal defense. All 21 Civil Air Patrol Coastal Patrol bases were abruptly discontinued on August 31, 1943. CAP personnel went back to their homes and their civilian professions. Many joined the regular military or volunteered to do other unarmed CAP services.

(78) 1967 CAP MONUMENT DEDICATION
by Rehoboth boardwalk.

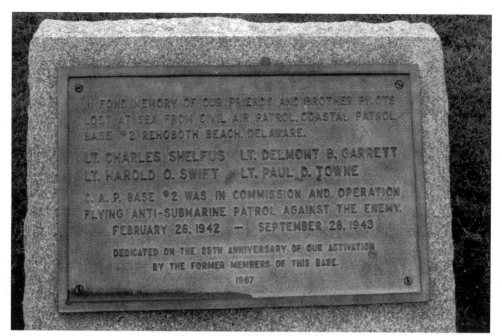

(79) REHOBOTH CAP MONUMENT.

(77) AIR MEDAL

AN AIR MEDAL BUT NO PENSION

CAP's signature ambiguity continued to plague it after the war. CAP Coastal Patrol personnel, referred to after their service, are usually called "veterans." But to the regret of many of their advocates, a more accurate title might be "former per diem contractors."

CAP personnel had signed up to be paid on a per diem ("by the day") basis. As World War Two moved towards conclusion, a campaign was created to establish military veterans' benefits, including pensions, for the Civil Air Patrol. This effort continued after the war ended.

It was finally decided to give CAP anti-sub pilots limited recognition. The quota of 200 hours of overwater flying was arbitrarily established as justification to receive an Air Medal from the U.S. Air Force, successor to the Army Air Forces. In 1948, ceremonies were held at or near the sites of all 21 Coastal Patrol Bases. *(Illustrations #75, #76)* But many felt the Air Medals *(Illustration #77)* were given to subdue the campaign for veterans' benefits, and that CAP personnel should have also received pensions.

However, unlike the regular military, Civil Air Patrol personnel had been free to leave their duty any time they wanted. The CAP veterans who qualified to receive Air Medals accepted them with dignity and the campaign for veterans' benefits died out.

Decades later, CAP's ambiguity surfaced again, and involved another pension issue. The Women's Airforce Service Pilots, (WASPs) had been another special civilian U.S. service of World War Two. They performed unarmed, but daring and valuable service, ferrying and flight testing military aircraft to free up male pilots for combat flying. After the war the WASPs also received no pensions. In the 1970s, a campaign was formed to procure limited benefits for surviving WASPs. In 1977, 33 years after their service had ended, the WASPs were given benefits. But as these benefits were given to the WASPs, there was reportedly concern among authorities that such pensions might also have to be given those who had performed WWII service with the Civil Air Patrol. The CAP veterans never received them.

(80) 2002 BASE TWO REUNION:
Front Row: Base 2 Veterans Arthur "Tom" Worth, Roland "Tom" O'Day,
Edmond "Eddie" Edwards, Glen Cook. Top Row: Author, and reunion co-organizer,
Roger Thiel, visiting CP Base 7 Veteran Clifton Bowes, Base 2 Veterans
Henry "Ed" Phipps, Maury Betchen, and reunion co-organizer Robert Cook.

(81) VETERANS HENRY "ED" PHIPPS AND EDMOND "EDDIE" EDWARDS
at 2006 roadside highway marker dedication. (CP Base 2, Rehoboth, Delaware)

VETERANS' REUNIONS

In 1948, as veterans of CAP CP Base Two gathered at the Rehoboth Airport for their Air Medal ceremony, they made the decision to subsequently hold annual reunions. They would be the only one of the 21 Coastal Patrol bases to do so. In 1967, at the 25th anniversary of their activation, surviving Base Two veterans dedicated a plaque to honor their four comrades who had lost their lives. *(Illustration #78)* It is placed near the city's boardwalk, at the end of Rehoboth Avenue. *(Illustration #79)*

Over the decades, these reunions, held in the City of Rehoboth Beach, Delaware, became a practical rallying point for historians and enthusiasts, and an irreplaceable resource for CAP anti-sub history.

Each year, Base Two veterans welcomed all interested parties into their midst and freely shared their memories of CAP anti-sub service as well as ongoing factors of their lives. At each reunion, a group photo was taken, often with the veterans sitting in front row positions of recognition. *(Illustration #80)*

In 2006, by the efforts of Base Two reunion organizers and the current-day CAP Delaware Wing, a roadside marker was placed near the former site of the Rehoboth Airport. *(Illustration #81)*

The roadside marker is located near the Rt. 1 Coastal highway about one and a half miles inland from the City of Rehoboth Beach. The marker is near a tall, modern communications tower. Turn south on Miller Road, proceed about 200 yards, then turn left on Airport Road. Proceed 150 yards and the plaque is on the left, directly across from the AmericInn Lodge & Suites, 36012 Airport Road, Rehoboth Beach, Del. 19971.

(82) ENEMIES NO MORE.
From left: CAP Veteran Edmond "Eddie" Edwards, CAP Veteran Roland "Tom" O'Day,
German Navy Veteran (U-373 Radio Operator) Fred Geils, CAP Veteran Glen Cook, CAP
Veteran Henry "Ed" Phipps (1992 Reunion, CP Base 2, Rehoboth, Delaware)

(83) 1992 REHOBOTH REUNION:
Former German Navy enemy, Fred Geils, front row, third from right.
Author, top row, second from right.

ENEMIES NO MORE

"He was just doing his job."

At their 1992 reunion, the Rehoboth CAP veterans welcomed a very special guest. *(Illustration #82)* Fred Geils had been the radar operator on the U-373, a German submarine which made World War Two combat patrols in American waters, including the Delaware coast.

On the night of June 10-11, 1942, the U-373 laid 15 mines about six miles offshore from Rehoboth Beach. During this time, Base Two personnel were flying continuous armed daytime missions against German U-boats. One mine laid by Geils's U-boat was contacted by an American oceangoing tugboat. The total destruction of the ocean tug, and all hands, was eyewitnessed by CAP Lt. Roland "Tom" O'Day on either June 11th or 12th, 1942.

Fifty years later, when Geils arrived at Base Two's 1992 reunion, he was understandably nervous as CAP veterans walked up to meet him. However, the first to thrust out his hand in friendship was O'Day, who said about Geils, "he was just doing his job."

Geils was welcomed to the group and included in the traditional annual group photo of veterans. *(Illustration #83)* This visit is believed to be the only meeting, ever, between veterans of the CAP Coastal Patrol and a former German enemy.

(Also see Illustration #24, Direct Eyewitnesses to War's Destruction).

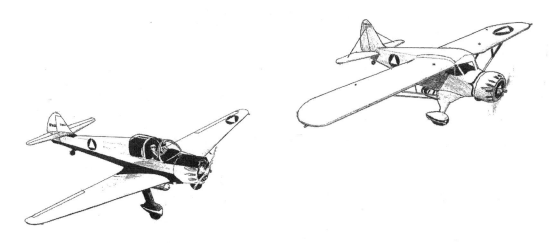

(84) RYAN SCW (LEFT) AND STINSON RELIANT ON PATROL
(Illustrations by Brian Hope)

AFTERWORD

Periodically uncovered but generally hidden, the Civil Air Patrol Coastal Patrol shines out, almost reluctantly, over the span of more than seven decades. It endures as an unsung, but glorious "nugget" of World War Two, the biggest event in world history. It presents an inspirational story of America and an emblematic piece of national history, almost entirely forgotten for decades and hardly known now.

WHY IS CIVIL AIR PATROL COASTAL PATROL SO LITTLE KNOWN?

All aspects of the war's Battle of the Atlantic, especially as it affected America's east coast, remain cloaked to this day in an "historical unconsciousness." It is difficult or impossible for most Americans to grasp that World War Two came to the nation's front door.

CAP's signature ambiguity may make it especially prone to this haze of memory. "One foot in and one foot out" of the regular military can too easily become "neither here nor there." The CAP Coastal Patrol was a superb deterrent force but had only a handful of interactions with enemy submarines. And, upon disbanding, there was no designated system to record the CAP's history.

WHAT WAS THEIR MOTIVATION?

It has been said of CAP's World War Two services that they extracted the "unpurchasable" from some very skilled and dedicated people. But the motivation of these "airborne minute men" can also be elusive.

The CAP Coastal Patrol was dangerous. It was unglamorous. Yet hundreds of Civil Air Patrol anti-sub pilots risked their lives daily, often flying in severe weather conditions that left the regular military grounded. CAP flew without any of the compensations usually associated with this level of service. They received no special flight pay, no real recognition, no exemption from the draft and later, no pensions.

At reunions, veterans did not discuss any prime reason for their involvement. CP Base Two Veteran Henry E. "Ed" Phipps, as featured veteran for the 2001 History Channel segment about CAP anti-sub, said: "About all we had in common was that we liked to fly airplanes." Like most WWII veterans, the CAP did not call attention to their service. They were certainly as patriotic as any other group.

One probable motivation: CAP personnel served with the primal identification of fighting from their own homeland. Daily, they could see exactly what they were risking their lives for, so rare for American combatants in modern times. In using familiar aircraft and flying skills, they performed real war duties while remaining in stateside America. There was some feeling of "Lemme at 'em!"

As the classic 1946 American movie, "It's A Wonderful Life" depicts World War Two, it includes the narrated line, "George fought the 'Battle of Bedford Falls.' " The film's "everyman" hero, George Bailey, is portrayed as remaining at home in small town America and functioning as an Air Raid Warden while his wife, Mary, performs war support work. This duty, as most of Bailey's life, is depicted as unglamorous but noble. Although most of CAP's activities were more physically active than air raid wardens, Civil Air Patrol personnel of World War Two can be seen in the dignified image of George and Mary Baileys.

HISTORY'S ACKNOWLEDGMENTS OF CAP ANTI-SUB

Major historians of World War Two and the Battle of the Atlantic have praised CAP's service. Celebrated U.S. Navy historian Samuel Eliot Morison wrote about CAP in 1947: "They were people who wanted to serve, not to gain." Michael Gannon, author of *Operation Drumbeat: The Dramatic True Story of Germany's First U-Boat Attacks Along The American Coast In World War II* (1990) said: "There are few finer examples in the war of civilian generosity and intrepidity than those found in CAP units."

Civil Air Patrol's most profound testament came from Henry H. "Hap" Arnold, Commanding General of U.S. Army Air Forces during World War Two, who wrote in 1947: "For one period – at the start of the war – CAP was the only agency that was able to take any real action toward controlling the submarine menace."

THE ULTIMATE RESULT: CAP COASTAL PATROL HELPED TO DRIVE THE ENEMY AWAY

Illustration #85 depicts a CAP Stinson Reliant aircraft immediately after dropping a bomb on a surfaced German submarine. It portrays the historical thrust of Civil Air Patrol Coastal Patrol but is technically inaccurate. CAP airplanes encountered surfaced U-boats very few times, mostly in the first months of their service, before they became armed. By the late Spring/early Summer of 1942, most CAP Bases were equipped with bombs and depth charges. But by then, the U-boats would not generally surface during daylight, substantially due to the CAP's presence itself.

(85) CIVIL AIR PATROL COASTAL PATROL ON THE ATTACK.
(Illustration by Brian Hope)

A comparison of the decline in sinkings and the activation of CAP bases shows the effectiveness of Coastal Patrol:

Allied Shipping Losses: *1942:* In January there were 11 sinkings -- in February, 25 sinkings -- in March, 33 sinkings -- in April, 24 sinkings -- in May, 52 sinkings -- in June, 35 sinkings -- in July, 20 sinkings -- in August, 3 sinkings -- in September, 1 sinking (there were none after September).

1943: In all of 1943 there were 7 sinkings
(TOTAL 211)

Activation Sequence of 21 CAP Coastal Patrol Bases: Base 1: Atlantic City, New Jersey, February 28, 1942 -- Base 2: Rehoboth, Delaware, February 28, 1942 -- Base 3: Lantana, Florida, March 30, 1942 -- Base 4: Parksley, Virginia, April 16, 1942 -- Base 5: Flagler Beach, Florida, March 11, 1942 -- Base 6: St. Simon's Island, Georgia, May 12, 1942 -- Base 7: Miami, Florida, May 13, 1942 -- Base 8: Charleston, South Carolina, May 23, 1942 -- Base 9: Grand Isle, Louisiana, June 25, 1942 -- Base 10: Beaumont, Texas, June 24, 1942 -- Base 11: Pascagoula, Mississippi, June 24, 1942 -- Base 12: Brownsville, Texas, July 8, 1942 -- Base 13: Sarasota, Florida, July 9, 1942 -- Base 14: Panama City, Florida, July 16, 1942 -- Base 15: Corpus Christi, Texas, July 20, 1942 -- Base 16: Manteo, North Carolina, July 21, 1942 -- Base 17: Suffolk, Long Island, New York, August 6, 1942 -- Base 18: Falmouth, Massachusetts, August 25, 1942 -- Base 19: Portland, Maine, August 18, 1942 -- Base 20: Bar Harbor, Maine, August 22, 1942 -- Base 21 – Beaufort, North Carolina, September 7, 1942.

The 21 CAP Coastal Patrol bases were activated from February to September 1942. Most began anti-sub operations from May to August.

The decline in sinkings substantially matches this activation sequence. During this period, patrols of the regular military did not increase. This comparison, plus the 1947 testament by General Arnold (see page 91), heavily validates CAP as a civilian force instrumental in driving a military enemy from U.S. waters. *(Also see map, Illustration #4).*

———

(*Comment:* It is the author's opinion that CAP's effectiveness was based on placing patrol aircraft over the ocean, armed or not, rather than the factor of them carrying bombs or depth charges.)

THE FINAL NUMBERS –
CIVIL AIR PATROL COASTAL PATROL

-- 21 Bases, activated from February to September 1942 -- Period of operation: February 26, 1942 to August 31, 1943 -- Missions flown: 86,685 -- Hours flown: 244,600 -- Estimated total miles flown overwater: 24,000,000 -- Subs sighted: 173 -- Bombs dropped on targets believed to be submarines: 82 -- Survivors reported: 363 -- Aircraft lost: 90 -- Survivors of ditchings at sea ("Duck Club" members): 112 -- Peak strength (all 21 Bases): 1698 personnel -- Aircrew rescued at sea: 129 -- Floating mines spotted: 17 -- Ships in distress reported: 91 -- Convoys escorted: 5684 -- Fatalities: 26

CONCLUSION

CAP anti-sub shines out as a model of efficient, civilian effort, uniquely adapted to armed actions and rising to this duty with enormous effect. The CAP flew armed missions in aircraft never designed for war. But their unusual, hybridized tactics strongly helped turn a strategic tide. In just six or seven months, they were instrumental in re-establishing an Allied presence over what had been the besieged American coast. Convoys sailed with less fear, and there was a feeling of reclaiming United States sovereignty over its own waters. We will never know how much blood and treasure -- of human lives and of Allied ships and their cargoes -- were saved by actions of the Civil Air Patrol.

The most glowing report of the effectiveness of CAP anti-sub may have come from a German submarine captain interviewed after the war's end. In recounting what he faced while waging war 3000 miles from home, in what to him was a submerged, perilous, desolate, and lonely existence, he concluded by describing the worst: "It vas dose #&!*@ little red and yellow airplanes!"

The CAP Coastal Patrol's last words on the subject might be those of Major George Haddaway, Commander of Base 10, Beaumont, Texas: "People don't change. I still believe in the volunteer spirit of America. It will always be there when needed."

THE RELEVANCE OF CIVIL AIR PATROL COASTAL PATROL FOR AMERICA TODAY

The historic thrust of CAP Coastal Patrol endures, over the span of more than seven decades, to our current day. Today, as the United States grapples with new types of hidden enemies, CAP anti-sub shines out as especially relevant. The service of these "airborne minute men" speaks to us as an historic version of homefront defense, homeland security, and anti-terrorism in the current-day United States. It provides an enduring example that civilians – even in the modern machinery age -- have a role in America's defense, and that the ultimate strength of a nation is in its citizens.

A MESSAGE FROM CAP COASTAL PATROL VETERANS

*The veterans of Civil Air Patrol Coastal Patrol have expressed their
specific wish that possible future depictions of CAP anti-sub
not exaggerate their actual interaction with U-boats,
such as by incorrectly depicting a two-way armed battle
between the CAP and an enemy submarine.*

TWENTY DISCUSSION QUESTIONS

(for students – intermediate – advanced)

SEVEN DISCUSSION QUESTIONS FOR STUDENTS:

-- Brave Civil Air Patrol Coastal Patrol ("anti-sub") pilots could have encountered an enemy over 500 times bigger than they were. *(See Illustration #21) Can you describe a time in your life when you had to stand up to something much bigger than you were, or when you were part of a group that did this?*

-- Although the stated adversaries of CAP Coastal Patrol pilots were enemy submarines, their overwater vulnerability was far more dangerous to them. *Can you describe a time in your life when you expected one issue to be your main confront but another factor turned out to be more serious?*

-- There are many types of bravery. *Can you compare the bravery, motivation and ideology of CAP pilots who flew far out over the ocean in single-engine airplanes to the same qualities in soldiers, sailors, airmen, or other troops of the regular military, including in combat?*

-- Although the strategy of observation may not be as dramatic as other wartime actions, the CAP Coastal Patrol used it with great effect. *Can you describe a time in your life when observation and vigilance had a strong effect on the outcome of a situation? Can you compare it to special reconnaissance in the perspective of today's special forces?*

-- Upon arrival at a CAP Coastal Patrol base, many pilots had experience flying with sophisticated instruments such as radio direction finders and artificial horizons. Some were surprised to find their CAP anti-sub aircraft not so well equipped. But they nevertheless adapted, and found their way over the ocean by primitive pathfinding. *Can you describe a time in your life when you had to leave technology behind and proceed by more basic means?*

-- CAP performed the duties of the regular military with much smaller airplanes. *Can you describe a time in your life when you planned for a large resource to perform a task but, by resourcefulness, accomplished it with a smaller, and possibly less expensive one?*

-- *Citizen-Defenders.* The CAP Coastal Patrol in World War Two can be compared to other times in history when a small group of citizen soldiers defended their homeland against an enemy force of the regular military. One prominent example, of course, would be the actions of American colonists against the invading British military during the American Revolution. *Can you describe other examples from world history where this type of effort took place?*

TWO INTERMEDIATE DISCUSSION QUESTIONS

-- *Homefront Defense/Homeland Security.* The CAP organized citizen-airmen, using machines never designed for war, to fly out over the ocean against a concealed foe whose targets were civilian shipping. *Although the Battle of The Atlantic in World War Two was part of a declared war, can you see in CAP's Coastal Patrol a version of what is now, especially for the United States, called "homefront defense" or "homeland security?"*

-- *Anti-Terrorism.* The Battle of the Atlantic in World War Two was part of a declared war, but some of its Allied victims -- civilian freighters and tankers -- were defenseless, and the submarines were, of course, concealed. *Can you compare the Civil Air Patrol's actions in this conflict, especially of observation and vigilance, to what is now, especially in the United States, called "anti-terrorism?"*

ELEVEN ADVANCED DISCUSSION QUESTIONS FOR MILITARY ROUNDTABLES

-- *Swords and Plowshares.* In a reversal of the famous quote of "beating swords into plowshares," the Civil Air Patrol, by using civilian airplanes to augment the work of the regular military, could be seen as "beating plowshares into swords." The regular U.S. military went to war in airplanes with names including Avenger, Devastator, Havoc, Marauder and Hellcat. CAP went to war in airplanes named Reliant, Model 24, Voyager, Sport Cabin, Cloudster, and others. Every airplane used by the Civil Air Patrol had been built to compete on the open commercial marketplace for discretionary civilian dollars, advertising that it could carry a bigger load for a further distance while using less fuel. The argument could be made that these commercial virtues were what made them so efficient for wartime anti-sub duty, in what could be called "capitalism defending itself." *Could the CAP's use of efficient civilian airplanes, therefore, be considered a time when the plowshare was* **mightier** *than the sword? Can you name other examples from history to which this distinction could be applied?*

-- *Joint Civilian-Military Operations.* The CAP's civilian-imaged effort to assist the military can be seen in the spirit of England's famed Dunkirk evacuation. There, most of a massive, retreating Allied army was saved in May/June 1940 when hundreds of small civilian boats evacuated over 300,000 troops from European waters too shallow for military ships. *Can you name other examples from history where joint civilian-military operations (modern term: "CIV-MIL") produced a critical tactical solution?*

-- *America's Smallest Bomber?* The CAP's fleet of anti-sub aircraft prominently included the Stinson Voyager *(See Illustration #12)*. With a gross weight of 1680 pounds, this aircraft carried a crew of two and a 100 pound bomb with only 90 horsepower. Even in the current-day era of

Unmanned Aerial Vehicles (UAVs), the smallest regularly-used UAV, the "Predator," has a reported gross weight of 2200 pounds. *Does the CAP's Stinson Voyager aircraft, therefore, in either its World War II era or in current day, qualify as "America's Smallest Bomber?"*

 -- A U.S. "home guard" functioning for the regular military. There have been many "home guard" stories in American history. But, in CAP's World War Two effort, much of the United States regular military forces were "away on campaign." *Can you describe other times in American history involving efforts of a "home guard" when defensive forces of the regular military were absent or operating with reduced numbers?*

 -- Did they go or did they stay? In wartime, there can be a perceived difference between those personnel who "go" to fight and those who "stay" at home. The CAP Coastal Patrol is at a unique fulcrum point for this scrutiny. CAP anti-sub pilots who flew out over the ocean might be given credit as those who did "go." And yet it could be argued that by performing these actions from stateside America, that they did "stay." *Did CAP anti-sub crews "go" or did they "stay?"*

 -- "Semi-military" terms. The Civil Air Patrol became an "auxiliary" of the U.S. Army Air Forces in April 1943. Other words for semi-military services could include militia, annex, posse, deputization, "the volunteers," the "home guard" and other terms. *Can you name other "semi-military" terms and services, especially of the United States?*

 -- Citizen-Airmen. The personnel of the CAP Coastal Patrol are compared here to full military groups, such as the Air National Guard, to be called by a relatively new term, "citizen-airmen." *Can you describe other examples from aviation history for which the term "citizen-airmen" could be applied?*

 -- Something small against something huge. CAP Coastal Patrol aircraft flew in possible retaliation against an enemy which could be over 500 times their size in an historic version of the "circumstance of lethality." *(See Illustration #21).* Another example from World War Two of such great differences in size between adversaries would be of the

destruction of the German battleship *Bismarck* in 1941. In that action, British military open cockpit, fabric-covered biplanes with torpedoes slung under their bellies, called Fairey Swordfish, disabled the rudder of the huge ship. This action triggered a set of circumstances which would lead to the sinking of the huge battleship. *Can you relate other examples from military or other history where something small prevailed over something many, many times its size?*

    -- U.S. citizens performing actions of armed force. All of CAP Coastal Patrol bases ceased armed operations on August 31, 1943. CAP's boating counterpart, the Coast Guard Auxiliary, *(See Illustration #72),* ceased their lightly armed operations against invading U-boats later that year. It is possible that since this time, no American citizens have been asked to engage in actions of armed force on behalf of the United States. (Exceptions to this might be of special intelligence or law enforcement personnel.) *Can you relate any other examples from American history in which citizens have performed armed actions on behalf of the United States?*

FOR SUBJECTIVE DISCUSSION:

    -- Could the Civil Air Patrol Coastal Patrol be the most unique armed action in U.S. history? There have been many armed wartime services for the United States and each is, of course, unique. But consider these factors of the CAP Coastal Patrol:

    -- The U.S. government gave arms to civilians. – Some CAP anti-sub pilots returned to their own homes after performing armed actions -- CAP anti-sub bases performed armed missions with a continuous civilian economic presence, by which CAP personnel could be called per diem ("by the day") contractors, so rare for those operating from U.S. soil. – CAP Base Commanders had no power of force over their personnel, even those who flew armed missions. -- CAP personnel received no official draft deferment. – All of the CAP, including armed anti-sub bases, operated under the jurisdiction of the Civil Aeronautics Administration

(CAA), the forerunner of today's Federal Aviation Administration (FAA). -- CAP anti-sub personnel purchased commercial aircraft insurance and medical injury policies to perform armed actions. -- Husbands and wives served together at armed CAP anti-sub Bases. – Personnel of the CAP, including Coastal Patrol, received no pension or status as veterans after their service. FOR GENERAL SUBJECTIVE DISCUSSION: *Could the Civil Air Patrol's anti-sub effort, therefore, be considered the most unique armed action in United States history? Can you compare it to other unique U.S. armed actions?*

FINAL DISCUSSION QUESTION:

-- Could an effort like the Civil Air Patrol Coastal Patrol happen again? Under what circumstances would the United States again ask its civilian citizens to engage in future actions of armed force?

ACKNOWLEDGMENTS

The first acknowledgment must be to the memory of the Veterans of CAP Coastal Patrol Base Two, Rehoboth, Delaware. After the war, they made the decision to hold annual reunions, becoming the only one of the 21 Coastal Patrol Bases to do so. These "Rehoboth reunions" provided the only practical opportunity for ongoing direct study of CAP anti-sub. This book could not have been written without the advice, support and friendship of the Base Two veterans, 1979-2012.

Honorary Master Editors:
Charles Compton, Col., CAP
Veteran, CAP Coastal Patrol Base 1, Atlantic City, New Jersey

Robert Mosley, Col., USAF, Col., CAP
Veteran, CAP Coastal Patrol Base 3, Lantana, Florida

Literary Review by:
Ronald A. Oaks – David Grant
Geoffrey H. Tyler

Historical Review by:
Sean Neal -- Robert Cook – David Cook
George Brizek -- Everett Bennett

Overall Editorial Assistance by: David Grant

ILLUSTRATIONS

Artist Brian Hope (Illustrations #13, 19, 21, 84, 85) was a CAP cadet in Massachusetts Wing, became a maritime professional, and now serves as the Director of the WWII Liberty Ship, John W. Brown, *based in Baltimore, Maryland.*

Library of Congress: Illustrations #1, #2, (p. 66), #72.

National Archives: Illustrations #20, #25, #67, #68

LT. HENRY W. HERBERT

Copyright Legal Advice:
Hall & Vande Sande LLC
Washington Area Lawyers For The Arts

OTHER ACKNOWLEDGMENTS:
Nancy Alexander, Rehoboth Beach, Del. Museum -- Harry Bridges
-- Clark D. Cloukey -- Laura Cook -- Lisa Cook
-- Gerry Counihan -- Roger Eastman -- Joel B. Hamaker
-- Lester E. Hopper – John & Ruth Keck -- Judy Knight
-- James Kovacsik -- Denver McPherson -- Spencer H. Morfit
-- Susan Neal -- Michael Pangia -- Vincent Pangia
-- Print Express, Inc. -- Stephen Rourke, Esq. -- Susan Staff
-- Mirwood Starkey -- Robin West

Graphic Design by: Lisa Monias, South River Design Team

ABOUT THE AUTHOR
ROGER THIEL

Hailed as the "keeper of the flame" of CAP Coastal Patrol history for decades, and often called its most knowledgeable authority, Roger N. Thiel joined the CAP in the 1960s as a cadet and learned to fly in the "last taildragger class" of aviation cadets using older style aircraft.

In 1977, as an antique aircraft enthusiast, he took renewed interest in CAP's origins of using civilian lightplanes against invading German submarines during World War Two. Upon learning that some former pilots of the CAP Coastal Patrol held annual reunions, he traveled to Rehoboth Beach, Delaware in 1979 to meet veterans of CAP CP Base Two. This began a decades long dedication to this little-known part of American history.

Thiel has met and interviewed dozens of CAP anti-sub veterans from most of the original 21 Bases. He has given historical presentments on this subject over 200 times. He conducted forums on CAP anti-sub at EAA Airventure at Oshkosh for 30 years, 1984-2013.

He was the featured historian for the 2001 History Channel segment on CAP anti-sub. Thiel owns a 1938 Ryan SCW which served on CAP anti-sub duty. His other works about CAP anti-sub include an adventure story, "Enemy On Our Shores," to be published in 2016, a completed feature filmscript and a full-length novel in progress. He is a 50-year member of Civil Air Patrol. Other interests include announcing airshows and other events, and community theatre and opera.

With this book, Mr. Thiel is pleased to introduce the term, "airborne minute men," as an alternative to CAP's well-known term, "flying minute men." For more information about Mr. Thiel's research and aviation activities, see www.RogerThiel.com.

Illustration: Author (L) with CP Base 7 Veteran Clifton T. Bowes in 2002.

COMING IN 2016 –

"ENEMY ON OUR SHORES"

AN ADVENTURE STORY OF "WORLD WAR II'S MOST IMPROBABLE AIR FORCE" – THE CAP COASTAL PATROL

WITH OVER 50 MORE ILLUSTRATIONS AND PHOTOS.

YOU ARE THERE – in a small civilian lightplane – never designed to hold the bomb now bolted underneath it – flying out over the dangerous world of the wartime Atlantic Ocean – far beyond any safety limit – away from technology and into a primitive, alternate world – of intense personal confront and classic overwater pathfinding – navigating in low visibility by "reading" waves and ship wakes – and searching restlessly for an invading German U-boat – by weight, over 500 times bigger than your aircraft.

A GRIPPING ADVENTURE STORY OF CAP ANTI-SUB PATROL, WITH MANY FURTHER HISTORIC OBSERVATIONS. (Con't.)

**AN ADVENTURE STORY, BASED ON THE TRUE FACTS OF
THIS UNEARTHED CAP HISTORICAL "NUGGET" OF
WORLD WAR II -- *ARMED CIVILIANS* -- LEAVING
TECHNOLOGY BEHIND AND FINDING THEIR WAY BY
PRIMITIVE NAVIGATION --- FAR BEYOND ANY SAFETY LIMIT
– *OVER THE DANGEROUS WWII ATLANTIC OCEAN!***

––––––––

Excerpts from the text of "Enemy On Our Shores" (subject to change):

Arching up in blunt civilian defiance, the Fairchild sits in its
tiedown space, recumbent on its tailwheel, as if with the flat objective
of conquering today's sky. Its bomb also slants up on line. The overall
image is like a boxer sitting at the corner of the ring, brooding and
dangerous, poised for action. The "uncle with the shotgun" is still a noble,
but jarring image.

* * *

We fly further out into the primitive, the sky a big blue canopy
over us, the day polished to a high glimmer. The ocean is a presence that
envelops everything. The sea extends to, and becomes, the very curvature
of the earth. We are not so much flying over the sea as we are contained
within it. The ocean glares up at us, stark and ageless. It is more than
huge. It is a relentless presence, an everything. It is just there. It just *is*.

* * *

This is an empire: an alternate world, huge and primal, raw and
fascinating. We fly over floating debris, leaping porpoises, discolorations
that might be whales or might be invading submarines, wisps of smoke on
the horizon, and "cat's paws" of terrified little fish. And all of this takes
place amidst the tiresome, jiggling images of the binocular lenses, a radio
with one channel, the immense chatterings of our Fairchild aircraft, and
the huge roar of the engine.

* * *

This is a mental game, a confront with self. Our danger requires extreme reserves of concentration. Again I strain to the dark surface below us. The ocean does not want to give up its secrets. This is a very serious game of hide and seek. And it is for "keeps."

* * *

As I push the stick forward into a dive, toward the slender shaft sticking up from the ocean, hero-images fling themselves to me: of a homefront guardian, galloping to war on his flying steed, now about to rid United States waters of a terrible, dark, vengeful killer. This marauding intruder that kills civilian ships will be destroyed, poetically, by a civilian.

* * *

With less than a mile of visibility, I strive to relate every wave-top-clue, every ship wake, to all others, as if on some enormous game board. Only the ocean buoys are stationary. This is a furious imposition of mind-data, extreme but exhilarating. The antiseptic lure of an instrument simulator, and its stale world of scopes and dials, briefly flashes across my mind but quickly passes. My own computation system is now vast, and in this primitive intensity there is a curious liberation. My thoughts and instincts are clean.

Our lives are of huge importance, or they are of no importance at all. Take your pick. Our here, raw survival is thrashed out as merchant mariners live in constant peril of a torpedo, fish flee for their lives from other fish, and one of the world's best aviators, Lindbergh himself, did not use fuel gauges. Our situation is primitive and dire, but in it, I feel a strange vitality. With this unique CAP duty, I have left behind a thousand lower versions of myself.

* * *

COMING IN 2016!

www.enemyonourshores.com

"The sword sung on the barren heath,
The sickle in the fruitful field:
The sword he sung a song of death,
But could not make the sickle yield."

-- William Blake

Not associated with the current-day Civil Air Patrol.

Not associated with any other CAP historical program.

Made in the USA
Middletown, DE
14 July 2016